BASS RECORDED VERSIONS

The Jimi Hendrix Experience

are you experienced

ISBN 0-634-00919-2

EXPERIENCE HENDRIX

"A JIMI HENDRIX FAMILY COMPANY"

EXCLUSIVELY DISTRIBUTED BY

HAL•LEONARD® CORPORATION

7777 W. BLUEMOUND RD. P.O. BOX 13819 MILWAUKEE, WI 53213

Visit Hal Leonard Online at
www.halleonard.com

Visit Experience Hendrix Online at
www.jimi-hendrix.com

Purple Haze

Words and Music by Jimi Hendrix

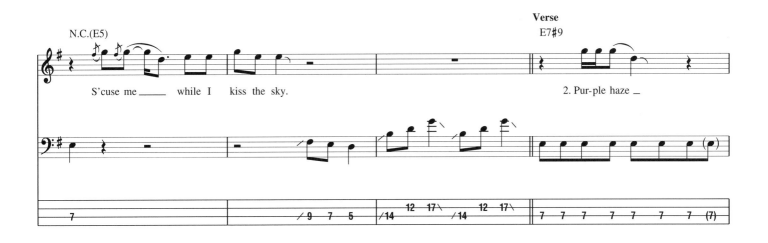

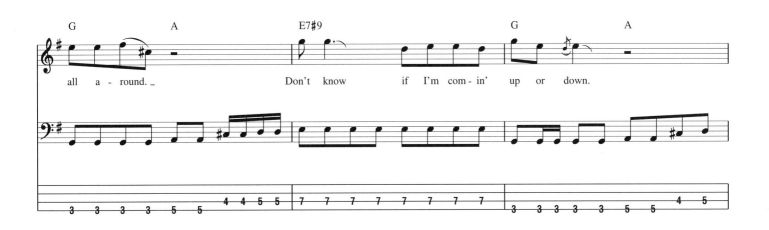

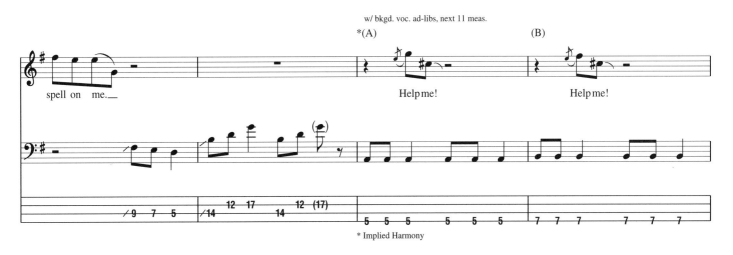

* Implied Harmony

Guitar Solo
w/ voc. ad-lib., next 8 meas.

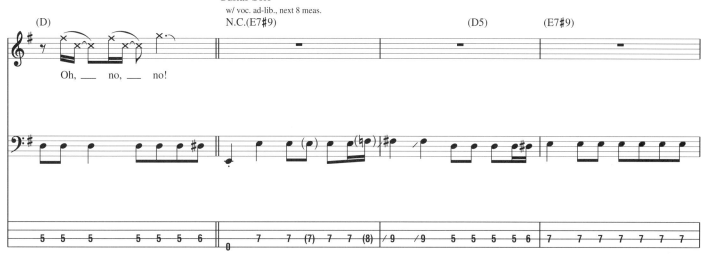

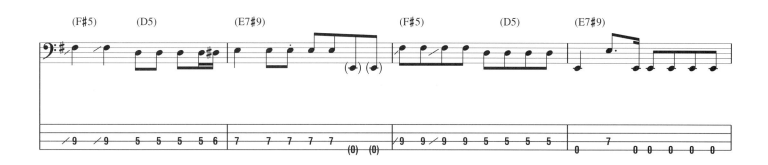

Interlude

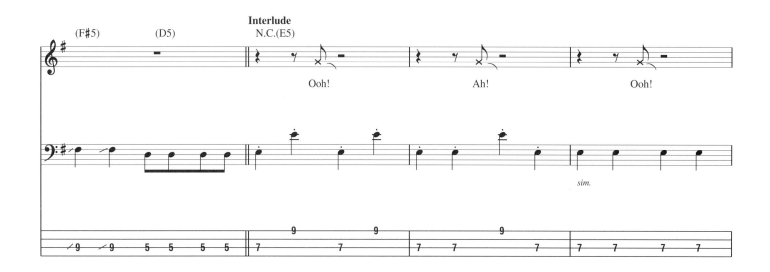

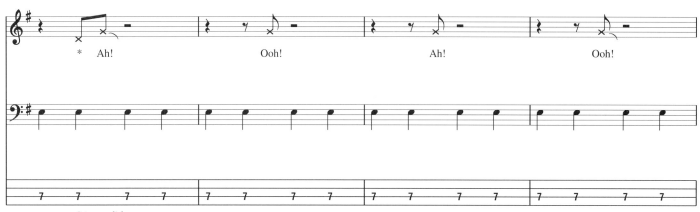

* tongue click

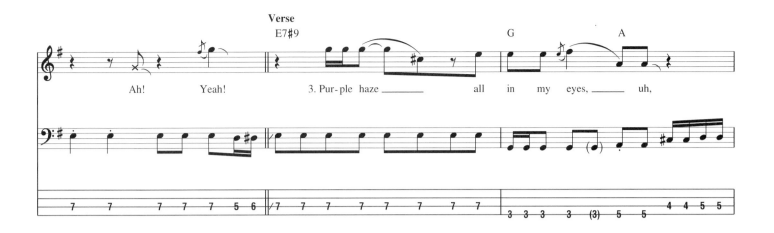

Verse

Ah! Yeah! 3. Pur-ple haze _____ all in my eyes, _____ uh,

don't know if it's _ day or night. You got me blow-ing,

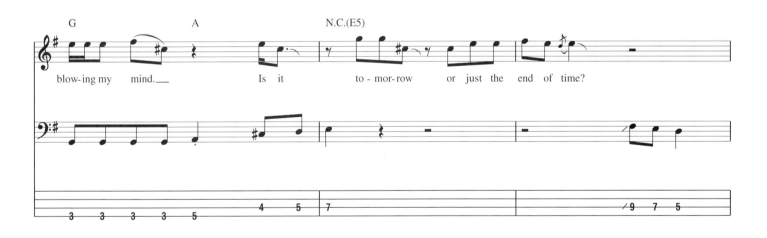

blow-ing my mind. _ Is it to-mor-row or just the end of time?

Outro

Ooh. _ Help me. Ahh, yeah. _____

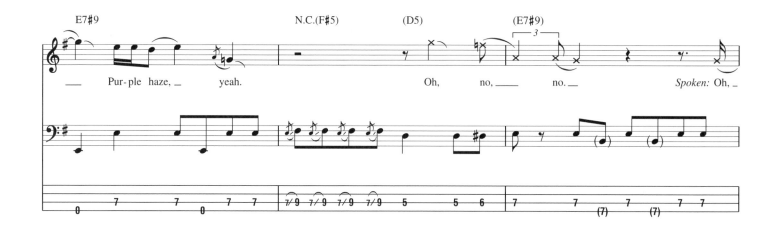

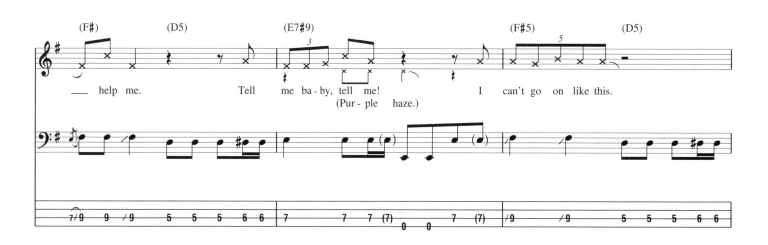

Manic Depression

Words and Music by Jimi Hendrix

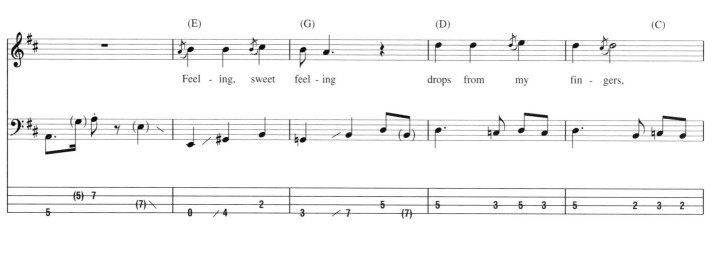

Feel - ing, sweet feel - ing drops from my fin - gers,

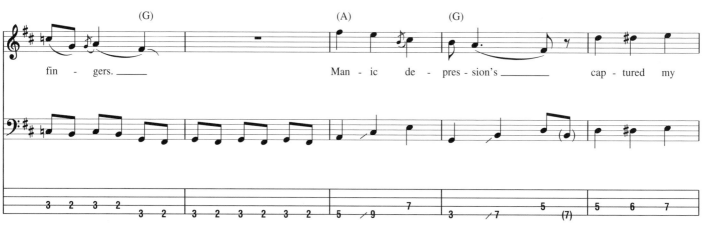

fin - gers. _____ Man - ic de - pres - sion's _____ cap - tured my

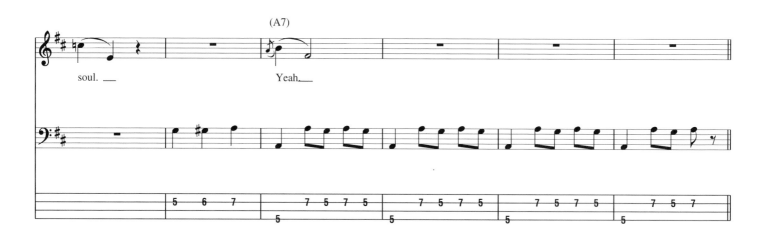

soul. __ Yeah. __

Verse

2. Wom - an so will - ing the sweet cause in vain. _____

Cry __ on __ gui - tar.

Verse

3. Well, I __ think I'll go turn my - self off __ and, uh, uh, huh, go on __

down. __ Huh! All the way down. Real - ly ain't no

use __ in me __ hang - ing a - round __ in, uh, huh, your __ kind of scene. _____

Hey Joe

Words and Music by Billy Roberts

22

Love or Confusion

Words and Music by Jimi Hendrix

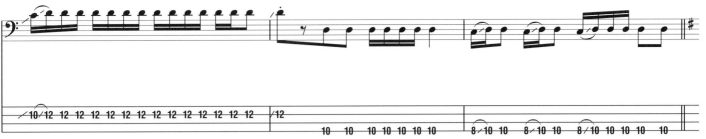

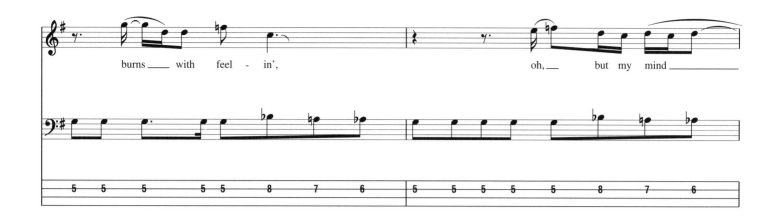

burns ___ with feel - in', oh, ___ but my mind _____

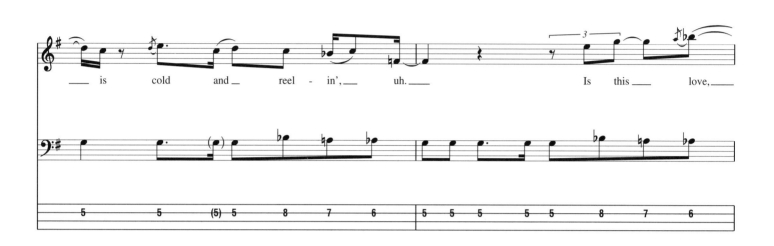

___ is cold and __ reel - in', __ uh. ___ Is this ___ love, ___

_____ ba - by, ___ or is it, uh, huh, just, _ uh, con - fu - sion?

Oh, ___ you tell __ me, ___ ba - by, ___ is this, _ uh,

uh, love _____ or con - fu - sion. _____

Ma - ma, we must get to-geth - er ____ and, uh, find out... _

ex - act - ly what we're try'n' to do. _____

Begin Fade   *Fade Out*

Whispered: Love _ or con - fu - sion...   con - fu - sion...

poco rit.

May This Be Love

Words and Music by Jimi Hendrix

with noth-ing else _ to _ do. _ So let them laugh, laugh _ at _ me.

Spoken: So, just as long _ as I have you _ to see me through, I have _ noth-ing to

lose, 'long _ as I _ have you. *rit.*

Verse

A Tempo

Bass: w/ Bass Fig. 1

3. Wa - ter-fall, _____ don't ev - er change _____ your ways. _____

Fall with me for a ___ mil-lion days, oh, my wa - ter - fall

I Don't Live Today

Words and Music by Jimi Hendrix

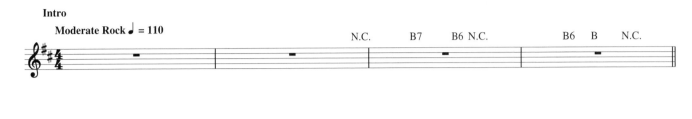

Yeah!

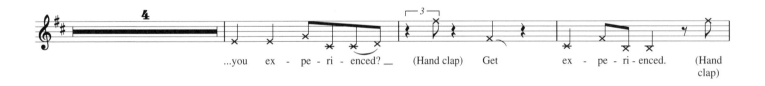

Oh, _____ there ain't no life ____ no - where. __

(Cough) Uh, hmm. (Laugh) Uh,   Yeah! __ hmm. (Sniff)   Damn, __ man.

...you ex - pe - ri - enced? __ (Hand clap)   Get   ex - pe - ri - enced.   (Hand clap)

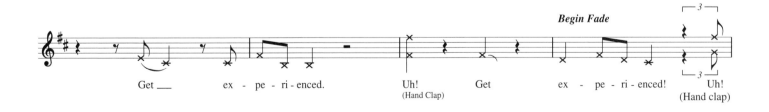

Get ___   ex - pe - ri - enced.   Uh!   Get   ex - pe - ri - enced!   Uh!
(Hand Clap)   (Hand clap)

Get   ex - pe - ri - enced!   (Hand clap)   Are   you ex -   pe - ri - enced?
Background: (You ex - pe - ri - enced?)   (Hand clap)   (Are   you   ex - pe - ri - enced?)

The Wind Cries Mary

Words and Music by Jimi Hendrix

Guitar Solo

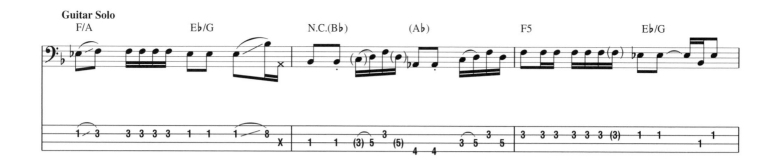

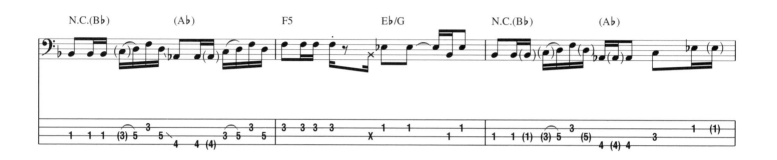

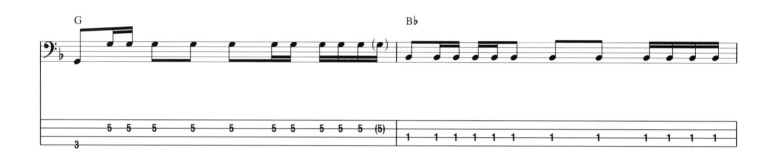

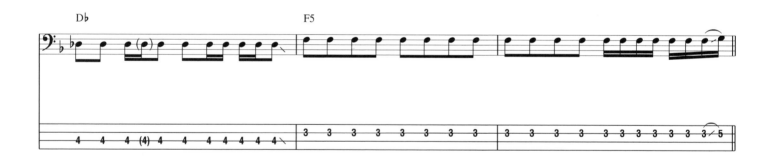

Verse

3. The traf-fic lights, they turn, uh, blue to-mor-row, ___ and

Fire

Words and Music by Jimi Hendrix

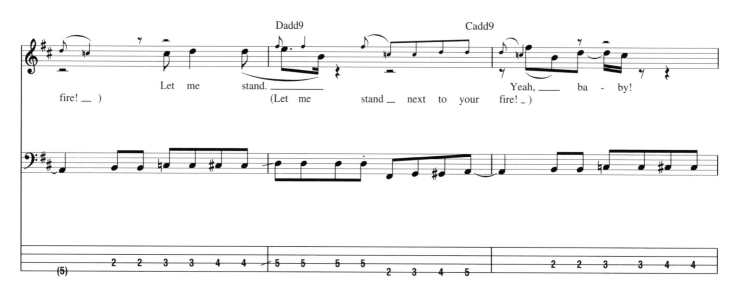

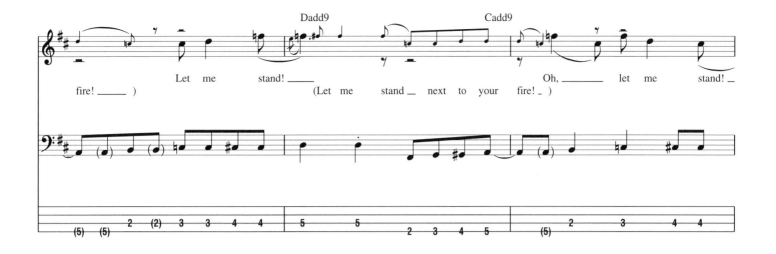

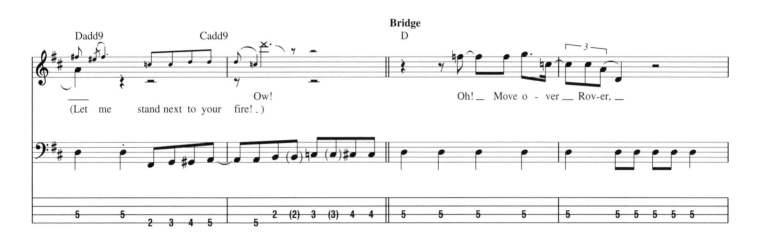

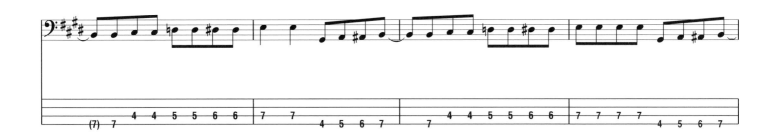

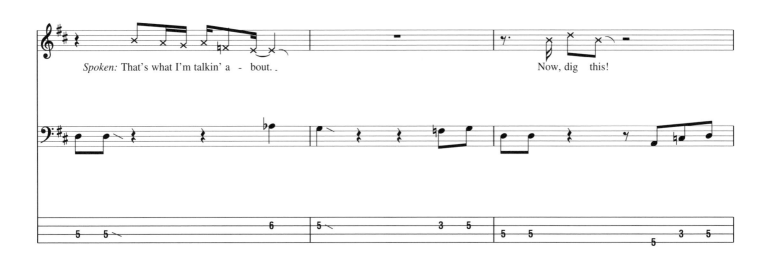

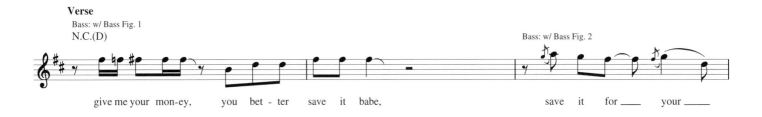

Third Stone From the Sun

Words and Music by Jimi Hendrix

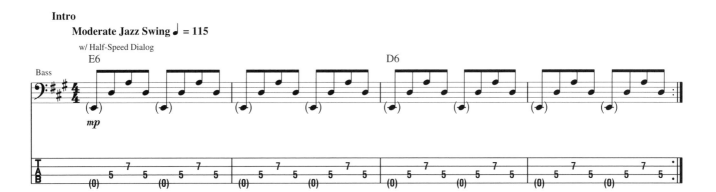

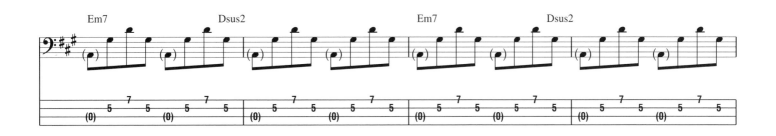

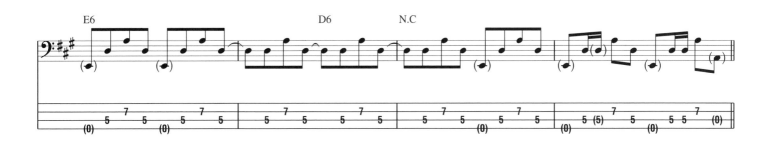

Interlude

Guitar Solo

Verse

Spoken: 1. Strange, beau-ti-ful, grass of green, with your ma-jes-tic ___ sil -

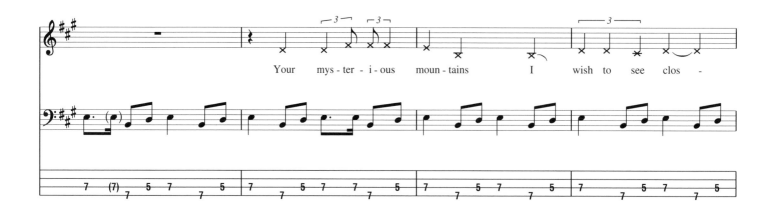

Your mys-ter-i-ous moun-tains   I   wish to see clos -

w/ ad Lib. half-speed vocal sound effects

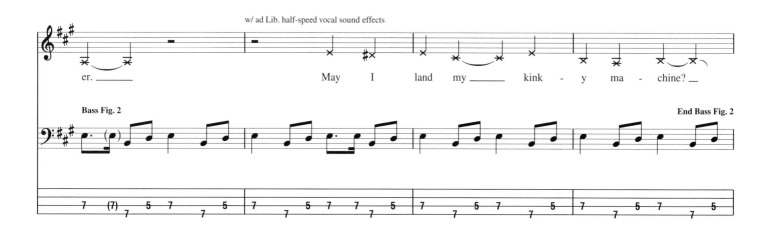

er. _____   May   I   land my _____ kink - y   ma - chine? _

Bass Fig. 2

End Bass Fig. 2

Bass: w/ Bass Fig. 2, 8 times

32

Bass

Verse
N.C.

Spoken: Al-though your world   won-ders me

Bass Fig. 3

End Bass Fig. 3

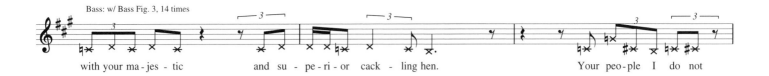

with your ma - jes - tic   and su - pe - ri - or cack - ling hen.   Your peo - ple I do not

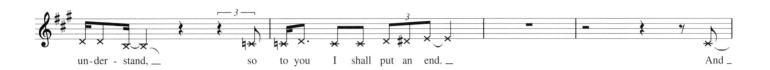

un - der - stand, __ so to you I shall put an end. __   And __

__ you'll   nev - er hear __   surf mu - sic a - gain.

w/ ad Lib. half-speed vocal sound effects

18

Theme
N.C.

play 12 times

Outro
  Free Time   In Time (♩ = 88)   *Begin Fade*   *Fade Out*

9

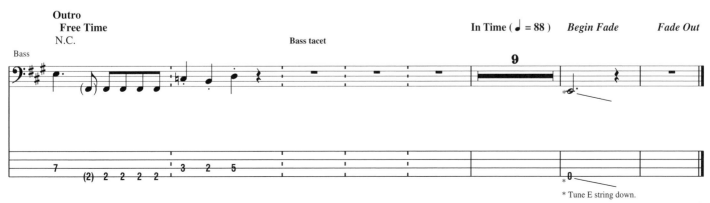

* Tune E string down.

Foxey Lady

Words and Music by Jimi Hendrix

* Key signature denotes F# Dorian.

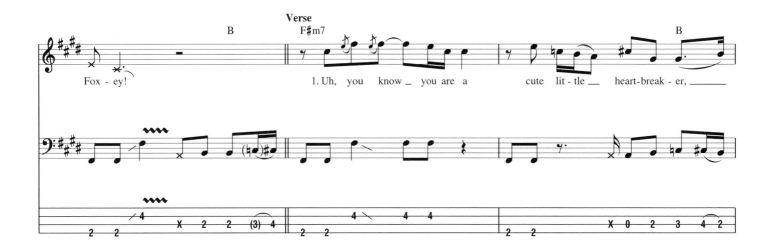

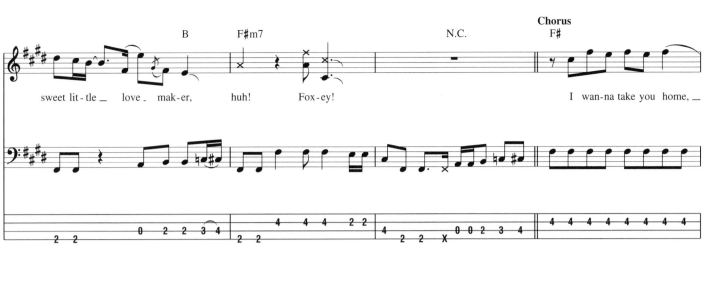

Are You Experienced?

Words and Music by Jimi Hendrix

Stone Free

Words and Music by Jimi Hendrix

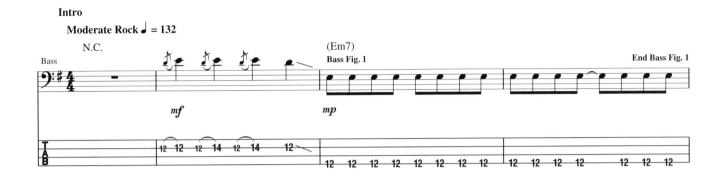

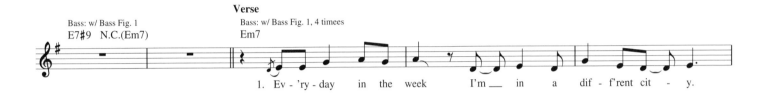

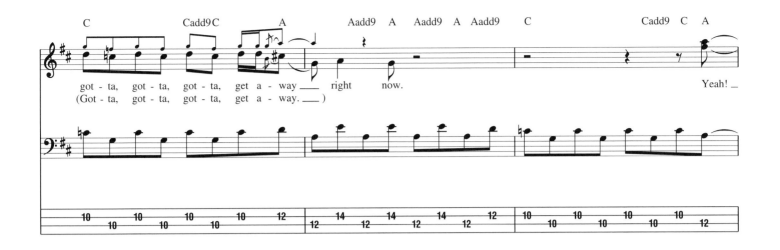

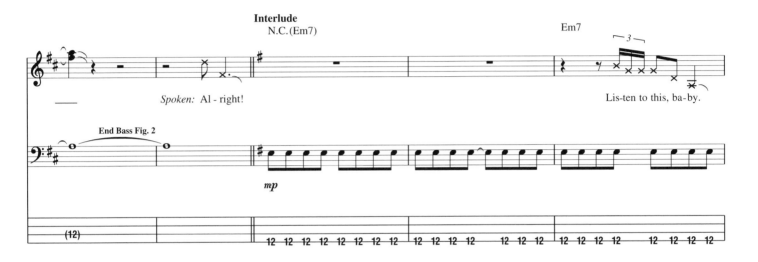

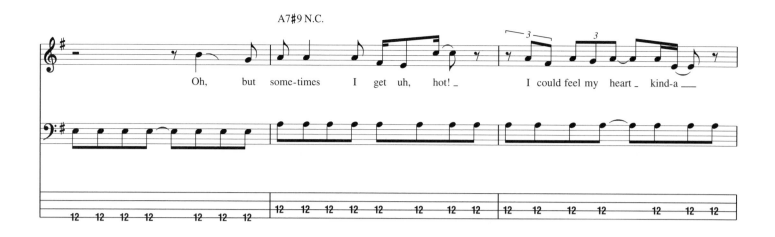

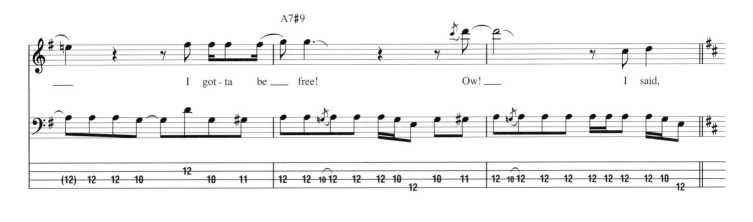

A7#9

I got-ta be ___ free! Ow! ___ I said,

Chorus

Bass: w/ Bass Fig. 2

| D | C | D | C | D | C | D | | C | D | C | D | C | D | | C | D | C | D | C |

Stone free, to do what I ___ please! Stone free, to

N.C. (D)   D   N.C.   D   N.C.

ride the breeze! ___ Stone free! I can't stay! ___

C   Cadd9 C   Cadd9 C   A   Aadd9 A   Aadd9 A   C   Cadd9   A

Got to, got to, got to get a - way! ___ Yeah! ___ Ow! ___

Guitar Solo

N.C.(Am)

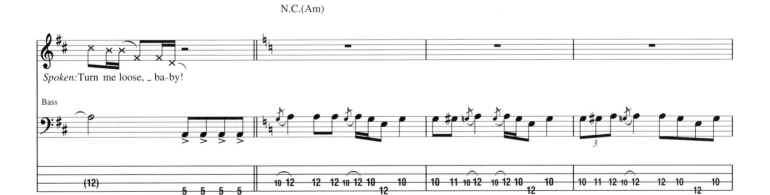

Spoken: Turn me loose, ___ ba-by!

Bass

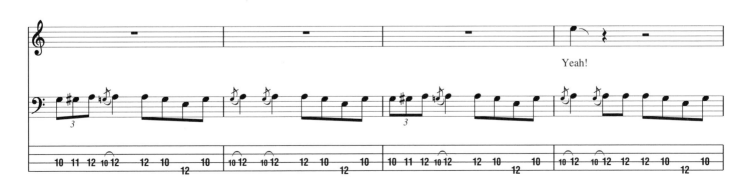

Yeah!

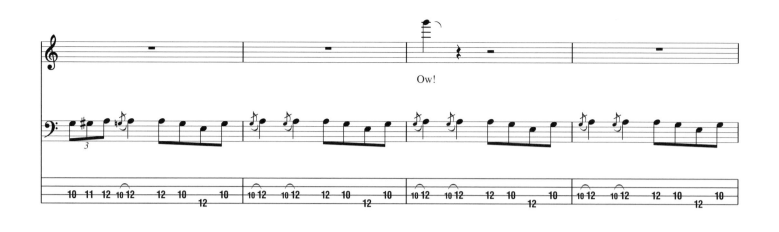

Ow!

Chorus

A7#9   N.C.   D   C   D   C   D   C

Uh, huh!   Yeah! _____ I _____ said, _____ Stone   free,   to

Bass Fig. 3

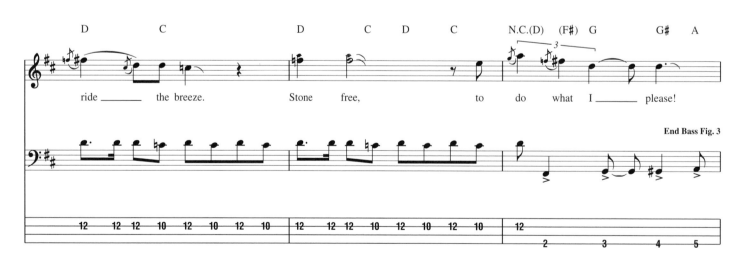

D   C   D   C   D   C   N.C.(D) (F#) G   G#   A

ride _____ the breeze.   Stone   free,   to do what I _____ please!

End Bass Fig. 3

Bass: w/ Bass Fig. 3, 3 1/2 times
D   C   D   C   D   C

Stone free!   uh, I can't stay! _____   I   got to,   got to,
                                                                    (Stone free!)

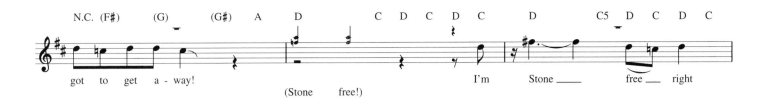

got to get a - way!
(Stone free!)
I'm Stone ___ free ___ right

now!   *Spoken:* Don't try to hold me back!   Ow! ___   I'm go-in' on down the high -
(Stone   free!)   (Stone   free!)

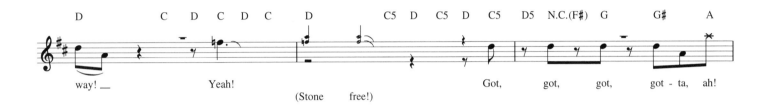

way! ___   Yeah!   Got,   got,   got,   got - ta,   ah!
                        (Stone   free!)

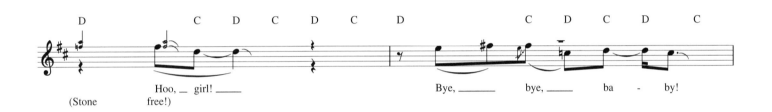

            Hoo, ___ girl! ___   Bye, _____ bye, _____ ba - by!
(Stone   free!)

            Ow! ___
(Stone   free!)

Bass

Begin Fade   *Fade Out*

51st Anniversary

Words and Music by Jimi Hendrix

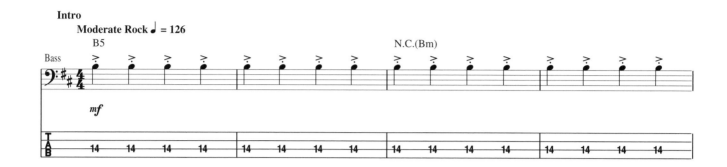

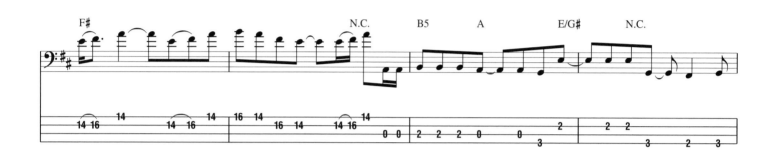

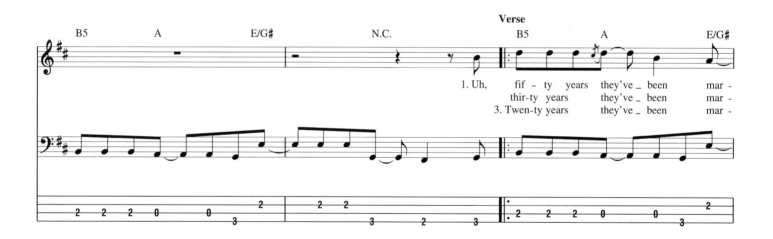

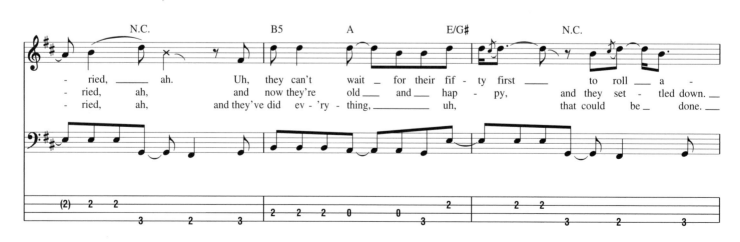

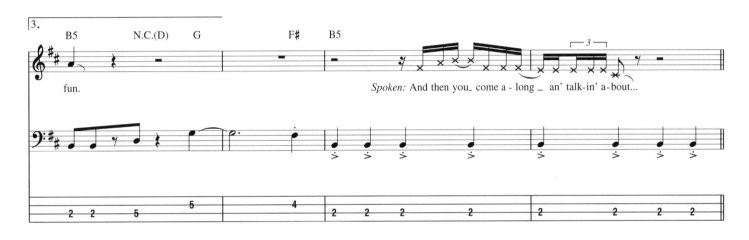

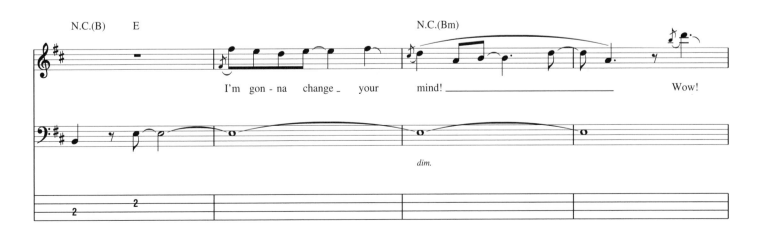

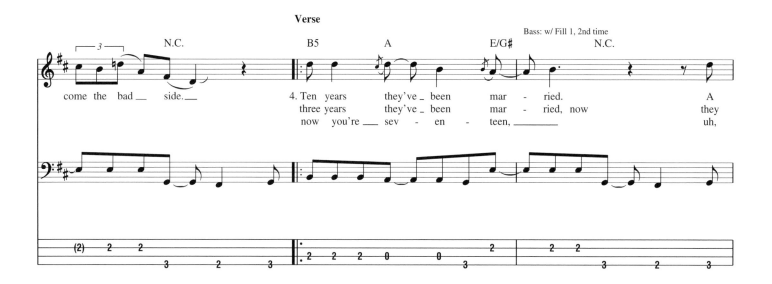

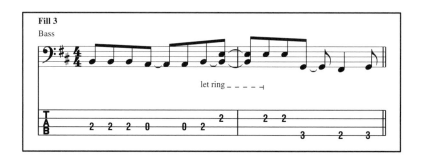

Bass: w/ Fill 2, 2nd time

Daddy's down at the whiskey house. That ain't all! 5. Uh,
She's got another lover. Huh! Same old thing. 6. So
for you has just begun,

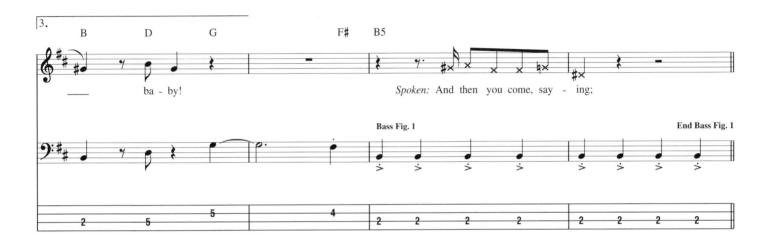

3.

B D G F# B5

baby! *Spoken:* And then you come, saying;

Bass Fig. 1

End Bass Fig. 1

Chorus

Bass: w/ Bass Fig. 1, 5 1/2 times

N.C.(Bm)

So you, you say you wanna be married. *Spoken:* Aw,

baby, try'n' to put me on a chain. Ain't that

Fill 2

Bass

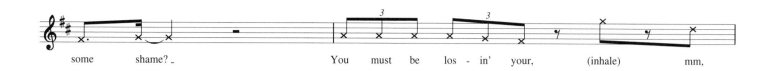

some shame? _____ You must be los - in' your, (inhale) mm,

sweet lit - tle mind! ___ I ain't read - y ___ yet, ba - by.

B5   E   N.C.(Bm)

I ain't read-y. ___ I'm gon - na change __ your mind, _____ uh!

Bass

dim.

2 0 2 0 2 0 2 0 | 2   2

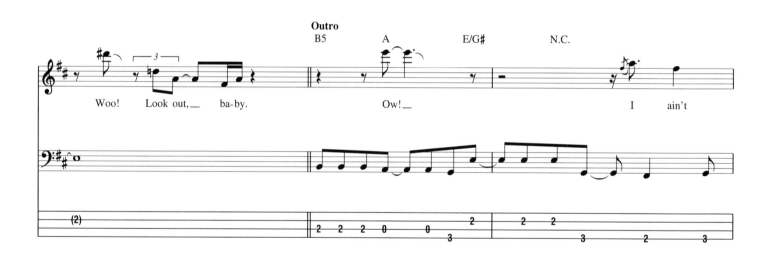

Outro
B5   A   E/G#   N.C.

Woo! Look out, __ ba-by.   Ow! __   I ain't

(2)   2 2 2 0   0   2   2   2
        3   3   2   3

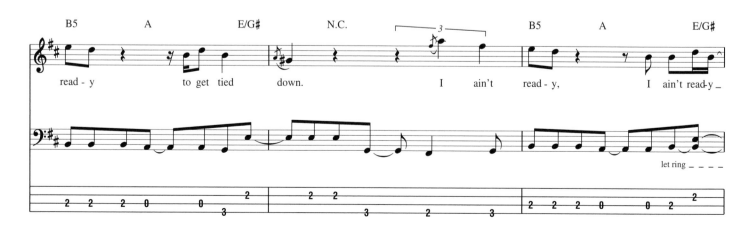

B5   A   E/G#   N.C.   B5   A   E/G#

read - y   to get tied   down.   I ain't   read - y,   I ain't read-y _

let ring _ _ _ _

2 2 2 0   0   2   2 2   2   2 2 2 0   0 2   2
            3   3   2   3   3

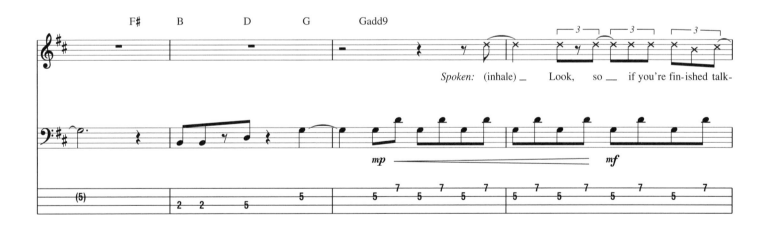

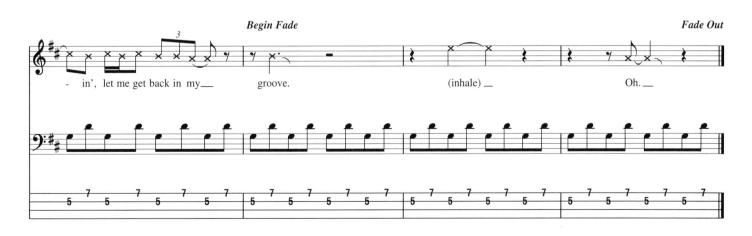

Highway Chile

Words and Music by Jimi Hendrix

Yeah!   Whoa! __

Guitar Solo
F♯

Yeah. __

One more __ com - in'! __

Verse

D7#9

3. His old gui - tar slung a - cross his back, __ his dust - y boots and Sears __

F#

__ Cad - il - lac. Flam - in' hair __ just a - blow - in' in the wind, __

Pre-Chorus
(♪♪ = ♪♪)
N.C.(A)

ain't seen a bed in so long, __ it's a sin. Now, you may call him a tramp, __

Can You See Me?

Words and Music by Jimi Hendrix

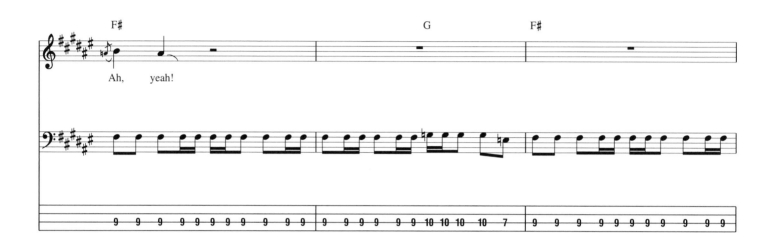

Ah,   yeah!

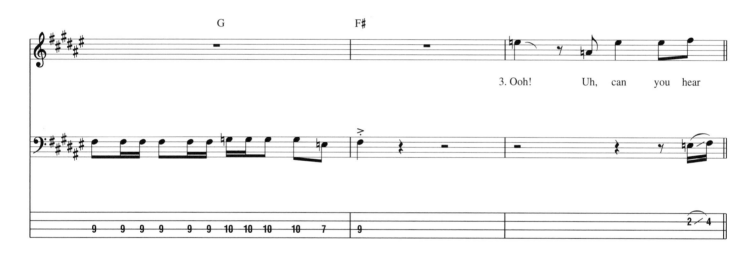

3. Ooh!   Uh, can   you hear

Verse

Bass: w/ Bass Fig. 1, 2 times

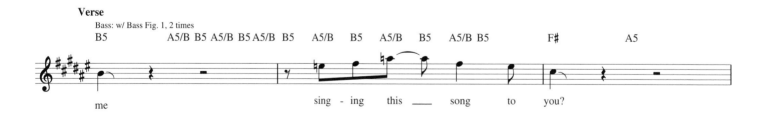

me   sing - ing   this ___ song   to   you?

Spoken: Ah, ___ you bet - ter o - pen up your ___ ears, ___ ba - by!   Can you hear ___

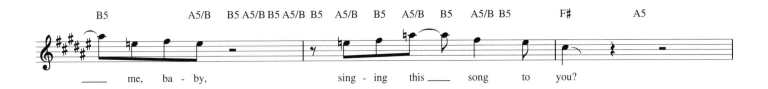

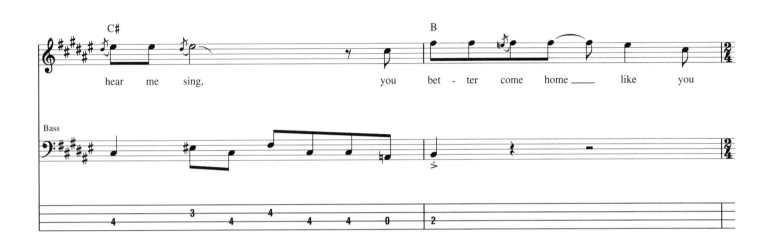

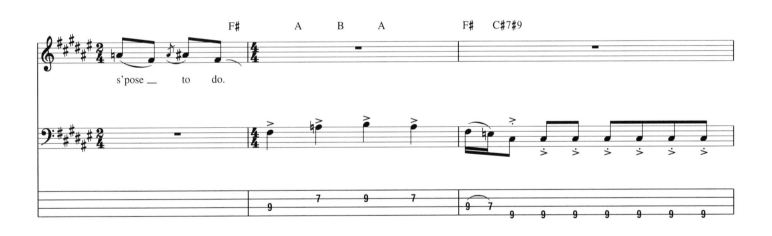

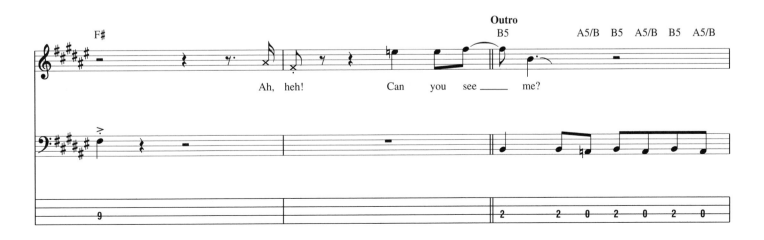

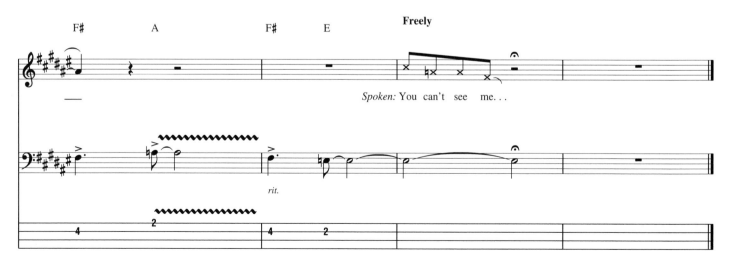

Remember

Words and Music by Jimi Hendrix

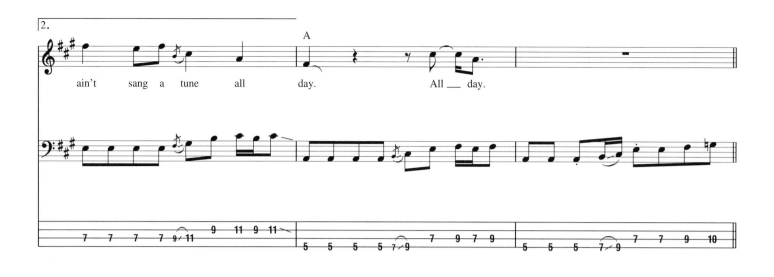

ain't sang a tune all day. All __ day.

Bridge

Hey, __ pret-ty ba - by, come on back to me, __ make ev - 'r' - bod - y

Guitar Solo

hap - py as can be, yeah!

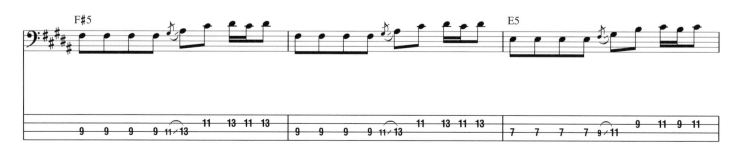

Verse

ba - by,   if   you please   come home a - gain, __   you know   I'll   kiss you for my sup - per.

Yeah.   You know   I'll   kiss you for my din - ner, ba - by, now. __   But, uh, __

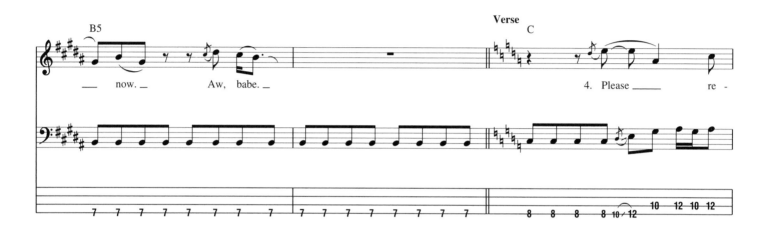

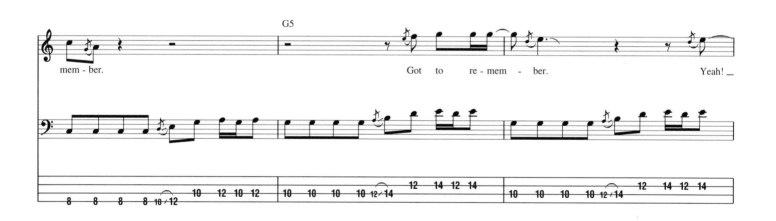

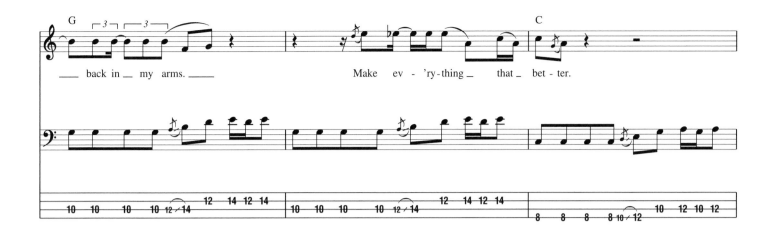

back in __ my arms. __ Make ev - 'ry-thing __ that __ bet - ter.

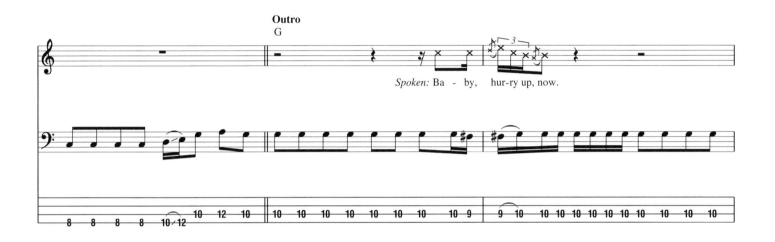

Outro

Spoken: Ba - by, hur-ry up, now.

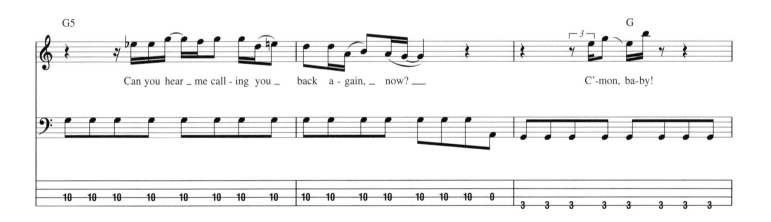

Can you hear __ me call - ing you __ back a - gain, __ now? __ C'-mon, ba-by!

Spoken: Stop jiv - in' a-round! Hur-ry home, _____ hur-ry home, __ uh.

Red House

Words and Music by Jimi Hendrix

Guitar Solo

Spoken: That's al-right, I still got my gui-tar. Look out, now! _

Yeah! _

That's al-right! _

Verse

3. Well, I might as well, uh,___ go back o-ver yon - der, _

way back a-mong the hills. *Spoken:* Yeah, that's what I'm gon-na do. Lord, I

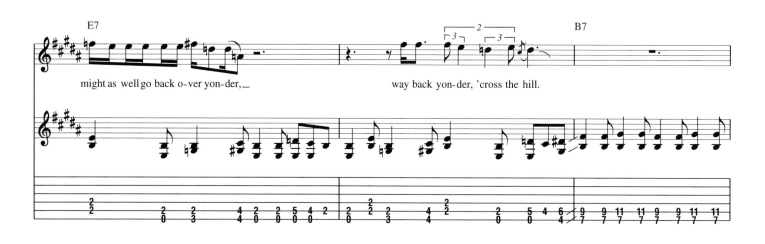

might as well go back o-ver yon-der, way back yon-der, 'cross the hill.

'Cos if my ba-by don't love me no more, I know her sis-ter will!

Free Time

Yeah!

Bass Notation Legend

Bass music can be notated two different ways: on a *musical staff*, and in *tablature*.

THE MUSICAL STAFF shows pitches and rhythms and is divided by bar lines into measures. Pitches are named after the first seven letters of the alphabet.

TABLATURE graphically represents the bass fingerboard. Each horizontal line represents a string, and each number represents a fret.

3rd string, open   2nd string, 2nd fret   1st & 2nd strings open, played together

HAMMER-ON: Strike the first (lower) note with one finger, then sound the higher note (on the same string) with another finger by fretting it without picking.

PULL-OFF: Place both fingers on the notes to be sounded. Strike the first note and without picking, pull the finger off to sound the second (lower) note.

LEGATO SLIDE: Strike the first note and then slide the same fret-hand finger up or down to the second note. The second note is not struck.

SHIFT SLIDE: Same as legato slide, except the second note is struck.

TRILL: Very rapidly alternate between the notes indicated by continuously hammering on and pulling off.

TREMOLO PICKING: The note is picked as rapidly and continuously as possible.

VIBRATO: The string is vibrated by rapidly bending and releasing the note with the fretting hand.

SHAKE: Using one finger, rapidly alternate between two notes on one string by sliding either a half-step above or below.

NATURAL HARMONIC: Strike the note while the fret hand lightly touches the string directly over the fret indicated.

MUFFLED STRINGS: A percussive sound is produced by laying the fret hand across the string(s) without depressing them and striking them with the pick hand.

BEND: Strike the note and bend up the interval shown.

BEND AND RELEASE: Strike the note and bend up as indicated, then release back to the original note. Only the first note is struck.

RIGHT-HAND TAP: Hammer ("tap") the fret indicated with the "pick-hand" index or middle finger and pull off to the note fretted by the fret hand.

LEFT-HAND TAP: Hammer ("tap") the fret indicated with the "fret-hand" index or middle finger.

SLAP: Strike ("slap") string with right-hand thumb.

POP: Snap ("pop") string with right-hand index or middle finger.

Additional Musical Definitions

 (accent)
- Accentuate note (play it louder)

 (accent)
- Accentuate note with great intensity

 (staccato)
- Play the note short

⊓
- Downstroke

∨
- Upstroke

D.S. al Coda
- Go back to the sign (𝄋), then play until the measure marked "***To Coda***," then skip to the section labelled "***Coda***."

D.C. al Fine
- Go back to the beginning of the song and play until the measure marked "***Fine***" (end).

Bass Fig.
- Label used to recall a recurring pattern.

Fill
- Label used to identify a brief pattern which is to be inserted into the arrangement.

tacet
- Instrument is silent (drops out).

- Repeat measures between signs.

- When a repeated section has different endings, play the first ending only the first time and the second ending only the second time.

NOTE: Tablature numbers in parentheses mean:
1. The note is being sustained over a system (note in standard notation is tied), or
2. The note is sustained, but a new articulation (such as a hammer-on, pull-off, slide or vibrato begins, or
3. The note is a barely audible "ghost" note (note in standard notation is also in parentheses).

Study the master with these transcriptions and explorations of the techniques and tunes that made Hendrix a legend.

Guitar Recorded Versions folios feature complete transcriptions for guitar plus rare photos and extensive introductions. Easy Recorded Versions feature guitar transcriptions with the harder solos removed. Bass and Drum Recorded Versions feature exact transcriptions for those instruments. Transcribed Scores feature note-for-note transcriptions in score format for *all* the instruments in each recording. All books include notes and tablature.

Are You Experienced

11 songs from the album including: Are You Experienced • Foxey Lady • Hey Joe • Manic Depression • Purple Haze • The Wind Cries Mary • and more.

00692930	Guitar Recorded Versions	$24.95
00660097	Easy Recorded Versions	$12.95
00690371	Bass Recorded Versions	$19.95
00690372	Drum Recorded Versions	$19.95
00672308	Transcribed Scores (17 songs)	$29.95

Axis: Bold As Love

13 songs from the album, including: Bold As Love • Castles Made of Sand • Little Wing • Spanish Castle Magic • and more.

00692931	Guitar Recorded Versions	$22.95
00660195	Easy Recorded Versions (12 songs)	$12.95
00690373	Bass Recorded Versions	$19.95
00690374	Drum Recorded Versions	$19.95
00672345	Transcribed Scores	$29.95

Band of Gypsys

Contains note-for-note transcriptions of: Who Knows • Machine Gun • Changes • Power to Love • Message of Love • We Gotta Live Together. Includes introduction and playing tips.

00690304	Guitar Recorded Versions	$19.95
00672313	Transcribed Scores	$29.95

Highlights from the BBC Sessions

Guitar transcriptions of 15 tunes taken from Hendrix's live BBC broadcasts. Includes: Day Tripper • Hey Joe • Hound Dog • I Was Made to Love Her • I'm Your Hoochie Coochie Man • Sunshine of Your Love • and more.

00690321 Guitar Recorded Versions $22.95

Blues

10 transcriptions of Jimi's most popular blues tunes complete with an extensive introduction and photo section. Titles include: Born Under a Bad Sign • Catfish Blues • Hear My Train a Comin' (Get My Heart Back Together) • Once I Had a Woman • Red House • Voodoo Chile Blues • and more.

00694944 Guitar Recorded Versions $24.95

Electric Ladyland

16 songs from the album, including: All Along the Watchtower • Have You Ever Been (To Electric Ladyland) • Voodoo Child (Slight Return) • and more.

00692932	Guitar Recorded Versions	$24.95
00690375	Bass Recorded Versions	$19.95
00690376	Drum Recorded Versions	$19.95
00672311	Transcribed Scores	$29.95

First Rays of the New Rising Sun

Matching folio to the new release featuring 17 songs whose creation spans from March 1968 through to Jimi's final sessions in August 1970. Includes 24 pages of color photos and extensive notes on each song.

00690218 Guitar Recorded Versions $24.95

The Jimi Hendrix Concerts

A matching folio to all 12 songs on the live album with authoritative transcriptions for guitar, bass, and drums with detailed players' notes and photographs for each composition. Songs include: Fire • Red House • Are You Experienced? • Little Wing • Hey Joe • Foxy Lady • Wild Thing • and more.

00660192 Guitar Recorded Versions $24.95

Radio One

A matching folio to all 17 songs on the album of Jimi's live radio studio performance. Includes authoritative transcriptions for guitar, bass and drums with detailed players' notes and photographs for each composition. Songs include: Hear My Train a Comin' • Hound Dog • Fire • Purple Haze • Hey Joe • Foxy Lady • and more.

00660099 Guitar Recorded Versions $24.95

Woodstock

Relive Hendrix's Woodstock performance with these 11 guitar transcriptions plus an introduction and photos. Songs include: Red House • The Star Spangled Banner • Villanova Junction • and more.

00690017 Guitar Recorded Versions $24.95

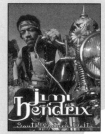

South Saturn Delta

Matching folio to the recent release of 15 tracks, including lost gems like "Tax Free," "Look Over Yonder," and "Pali Gap," as well as previously unreleased recordings like "Here He Comes (Lover Man)," "Message to the Universe" and "Midnight Lightning," and more.

00690280 Guitar Recorded Versions $24.95

Experience Hendrix – Book One Beginning Guitar Method

by Michael Johnson

This book/CD pack has been designed to guide you through a step-by-step process of learning music and guitar basics using the songs of Jimi Hendrix! It teaches guitar basics, music basics, music/guitar theory, scales, chords, transposing and progressions, basics of songs, blues, reading music and includes guidelines for practicing, tips on caring for your guitar, and much more. The accompanying CD includes actual Hendrix tracks to practice with, and on-line support for the method is provided by the Experience Hendrix website.

00695159 Book/CD Pack $14.95